World Poetry Symposium 2024

Poets Across the World

Ukiyoto Publishing

All global publishing rights are held by

Ukiyoto Publishing

Published in 2024

Content Copyright © Ukiyoto

ISBN 9789362699435

All rights reserved.

No part of this publication may be reproduced, transmitted, or stored in a retrieval system, in any form by any means, electronic, mechanical, photocopying, recording or otherwise, without the prior permission of the publisher.

The moral rights of the author have been asserted.

This is a work of fiction. Names, characters, businesses, places, events, locales, and incidents are either the products of the author's imagination or used in a fictitious manner. Any resemblance to actual persons, living or dead, or actual events is purely coincidental.

This book is sold subject to the condition that it shall not by way of trade or otherwise, be lent, resold, hired out or otherwise circulated, without the publisher's prior consent, in any form of binding or cover other than that in which it is published.

www.ukiyoto.com

Contents

Poetry by Riddhima Sen	1
Poetry by Sabbani Laxminarayana	4
Poetry by Rhodesia	11
Poetry by Revathi Raj Iyer	21
Poetry by Sankalita Roy	26
Poetry by Manmohan Sadana	42
Poetry by Kamalika Bhattacharya	47
Poetry by Aurobindo Ghosh	57
About the Poets	*73*

Poetry by Riddhima Sen

Faded Dandelions

My love, do you still remember
The days of explicit bliss;
When we were companions,
Bosom companions who could never be separated.
Lovers for an eternal timespan,

I still remember,
The warm smell of your blue cotton t-shirt,
The comfortable space in the lawn
Where we used to talk our hearts out,
Now, you have abandoned me
We may never be united again,
But, the memory of the sultry evening
Clinging to the fabric of your nylon cardigan
My pink sweater,
Continues to be persistent
Down my memory lane
The elegant view of the cherry blossoms
Strewn in my heart,

Light pinkish speckles
On my bleeding heart,
People go away,
But memories remain.

Although my heartstrings are baked with blood,
And embellished with the innards of my faint heart
I still cherish the memories of La Amour.
The dandelions have faded, beloved
White and shrunken.

Poetry by
Sabbani Laxminarayana

That is Love

How the oceans were formed is not known

Perhaps they are the tears of lovers!

That's probably why they are salty!

Make friends with your heart

Love honestly, innocently

Not being stable like trees or bushes

Maybe for having a mind, maybe for being human

Probably because they are intelligent beings and not like animals

Tears flow!

These seven seas were formed with those tears!

No matter the continents, no matter where people are

For having hearts and minds

For thinking that friendship should be not only friendship but also love

Maybe you won't find love in life

Hearts are broken

Tears rained down

Flowing in rivers

The seas have been formed

Innocent, crazy, cowardly lovers

Those who don't know that butter will come only if you cross your fingers !

"Always a train we have to get on

A lifetime late"

According to the words of the poet Arudra

What is the use of holding the leaves after burning the hands?

That's why cowards should probably not love!

Love demands sacrifice

For what and for whom?

Deva Dasu shed tears like a coward

Like Parvati, you have to spend time pulling the cart of life

Yes! Let's go, let's live together

Don't have the courage to?

Be it caste, religion, status,

Job, America, Australia,

Parents, relatives, friends, society

When there is a society of people who scream and shout

The ethics of arrogant and vicious scumbags

Because of the barriers of rules and regulations

Lovers have to cry like this!

Devadasa Parvati is an example of timid lovers

Laila Majnulu, Juliet Romeo

All the love stories are the same even across the continents!

Whatever the country, whatever the region

Lovers are cowards !

They think that if we can't live together, we will probably die

The name of sacrifice is given to it!

A blooming flower, a growing tree aspires to progress

What can you do if you are worried that you are not getting it?

Fools who think death is the way, cowards are lovers

Prepare to die!

Love is for giving, maybe not for taking!

As trees give flowers and fruits

As rivers and seas give water

People should give love!

Want unrequited love!.

When the wall of caste is put across love,

When the mask of religion is removed

Man is forgetting the relationship that is humanity

Love! Why are you born?

Love! Why are you dying?

Love is probably a giver not a taker !

We should love man as we love God and country!

Maybe give and forget!

Satisfaction Is there in giving!

As trees give flowers and fruits

As rivers and seas give water

People should give love!

Maybe love is the fuel for a man's life!

There is probably no man who cannot love!

Someone, somewhere will surely love someone

If love is one bond in life, marriage is another bond

A bond that binds love with marriage

It gives beauty and happiness!

Love is different, marriage is different for some people?

To hide the heart, to defile the mind

They are responsible for their own lives

Don't mask love, don't pollute love

That love does not come to cowards

Show the world and say!

Why cry and die?

It is to live, not to die to live

If not one, then another

A man can love one or two

If there is no impure mind

As the radiating sunlight spreads in all directions

We can spread our love to many people

Why suffer?

Do not suffer!

Time gives man some opportunities

It is the task of the wise to make good use of them

For not doing what should be done at the time it should be done

Time will do that work!

Yes, these people are leather dolls

Someone will play them !

Some lives are destroyed because they are creatures in their hands

Life remains as tears

Rather than living with money and status

Blessed are those who live with love!

Nature gave man a mouth to express his pain

Do people deceive the mind?

Self-witness knows the truth!

Ignorant lovers!

We are the creator of our life

We have to make our life like a beautiful garden or a beautiful world!

What is lost in life?

What we get, what we lose!

As the essence of Bhagavad Gita says

Transformation is the virtue of life!

If the nest collapses, it can be built again

The bird gathers and rebuilds its shattered nest feather by feather

Is it difficult for us humans?

To make this life beautiful and enjoyable

It is enough to find a man with a heart

Life is blessed!

That is love.

Poetry by Rhodesia

Ode to Papa

A decade has swiftly flown,
Since you breathed your last
And eased to eternal repose.
But the strum of your guitar
And your mesmerizing tenor
Still reverberates in our home,
With your heartening rendition
Of *No Other Love*, a vision
That had shaped my soul.

I take pride that I am your fruit,
You, an honest, noble man
Dedicated to your profession,
You have sailed oceans,
Reached far-flung destinations,
Even battled an iceberg,
As your ship blazed in flames;
Pouring all your strength, wit and passion,
You brought passengers safely home.

I have seen you pamper my mother
Like a queen, bringing her gifts from afar,
You fortified our home in caring patience,
Now, your secured, jovial clan has grown,
Each person carrying your essence,
And the blessings to your line bestowed,
Because of your righteousness and fortitude.
Beloved Papa, you will always be remembered
With warmth, reverence and gratitude.

Seventy-Five

You look as fabulous as ever,
No less beautiful as when
You cradled me in your arms,
Or held my hand to preschool,
And braided my teenage hair.

Your smile has never dulled,
Nor your eyes lacked luster,
For overflowing from your heart,
Is an everlasting spring of love
Resonating in your laughter.

Yours is a life well-lived,
Your crown is your wisdom,
Your children and our children
Adorn your scepter,
Our dearest Queen Mother!

The Tiger and the Lamb

You may not have sparked
The embers in my heart
Or ignited a fire in my soul…

So many times I questioned
The prank of fate
In joining our lives to woe.

How can a tiger
Live peaceably with a lamb
In one home?

Except to protect fiercely,
And flood the family
With food from your game.

I may be too scared
To even touch
The tip of your claws…

But I will mend
All your wounds,
And heal your pain.

Medgate

It is a company of healers,
A group of people who assure
To always be there
Whenever the sick need a cure.

Creating bridges
From the sickbed
To their treatment,
At the safety of home.

It is a gate that opened
An access to healing,
Once only imagined,
Now continually serving.

Bonds

He makes her smile,
An understanding friend,
Who lifts the veil
Of her predicament.

He warms her heart,
With soothing songs,
And vibrant dances,
Dissolving distances.

He feeds her breakfast
From the toil of his hands,
And builds a solid roof
To weather and withstand.

Which bond remains,
Which bond strains,
Which bond will last,
Which bond outlasts?

Long Ago

Long ago,
I have let you go
Free as wind.

I value you,
Sans strings fastened
To puppet.

Should you choose
A separate path,
I won't obstruct.

All rivers run
Their tortuous journey
Back to the sea.

Orbits

We are Mars and Venus
With the Earth in between us.

Our gravity doesn't matter,
Albeit attracted to each other.

For we have parallel orbits
That may never intersect.

Both dazzling on its own,
But mesmerized by the other.

Content on doting from afar,
To maintain law and order.

Poetry by Revathi Raj Iyer

Silence Of The Valley

"When life throws lemons, a poem also happens."

Poems are a beautiful way of expressing one's innermost thoughts, without any inhibitions. They have passion, truth, mystery, melancholy and sensitivity. A poem that kindles one's buried, treasured memories and makes a person hum, laugh, cry, dance or just smile, is priceless.

My poem is about a grave digger longing for his friend, lost in the abyss, and whose memory haunts him.

This poem is loosely based on the militancy in Kashmir.

***

Silence Of The Valley

The gorgeous ravines resonate the sound of silence

The ghosts of the kindred, haunt in the dead of the night

A cold darkness fills a dread in me

I shudder, as I think of my friend.

His soulful music caressed the cool breeze
A melancholy in every strum
His music reverberates in my ears
Alas! Fills me with sorrow, profound.

We grew up here, amidst cloaked innocence
Watching the clouds descend like a blanket
To protect us, the hills and the valley.

The sunshine kissed the mountains
The moonlight shimmered over the valley
A poet rose within me
As the beauty overwhelmed my senses.

My home was a heaven, once
Now, a graveyard warped with time
I emerge as a grave digger
Knew not why my destiny was so.

Why did I not run away?

Did hope fail me?

I am too depressed and drained
To even think straight
The poet in me died slowly
I live in the shadow of ghosts.

Oh! My beautiful home
God's own creation
Humans have torn apart
Turned it into a living hell.

Memories! An echo from the past
Cannot be erased.
One can dwell or revel in them
Or let them rest in peace.

I live in the here and now
And that will also join the memory wagon
In the blink of an eye.

Memories! Emotional props that sustain us.
Could we live without them? Beyond them?

I long for my dear friend, his soothing music
"Will I ever see him again?" I wonder…
"What lies beyond the hills?" I wonder…

Poetry by Sankalita Roy

Goody-Girl

I'm an example of good girl

Whose silence is appreciated by all

I'm an example of report cards

Filled with lack of confidence

I'm the one whose innocence is admired

Whose maturity is the hated attribute

I'm the one whose shoulders are filled with expectations

Of heavy bags that are meant to be carried everywhere

I'm the live example of regret

For doing too much for others

Instead of myself

I'm the one person who isn't smart

But patient way too much

Whose voice hardly heard

Whose silence always misunderstood

Whose love always taken advantage of

I'm the example of a goody-girl

Who refused to be the one

I'm the example of clay that cannot be molded
In a pot full of water.

Room full of coils

It is as if my mind is a coil
Full of other coils
Completely entangled into one another
If you try to remove the red ones from the blue
All of them coils further
Further down the line the coil
Making the room around me as dark as coal
With no stars in the sky above
One who cannot use the moonlight as well
The coil opens one by one
But they entangle my hands now
I try to free myself but I catch the cold from it
I try to run but it's pulling me back
In the most unanticipated situation, I stay silent
Sit down for a while
Wonder if what I did is really worth or not
Like all the other times, I roll
The tickets of my busfare
I do something same in the darkness of the room

When out of nowhere the coil detangle me,
I run but I sit down
I see a light at the furthest side of the room
I laugh and I run.

Deepest Retrospection

I woke up from a sleep in September
On a warm shiny summer day
All I thought to myself
I could have all I need
In this world of warmth and willingness
I sit down once again
Soaking my feet in the shining sun
I listen to the honking of the cars
I listen to the mother next door
All I do is wonder
Wonder in the wide world
As a long leisured lady
If all I can do is think
When will I live?
When will I enjoy the fruits?
Of all the years of thinking
I took out my feet
To climb out of my chambers
I cry a bit to myself

As my heart hurts the most
With various voices around me
I dry the tears, I put on a smile
I laugh to the world outside me
Like the fierce flames of the sun
The world mistook me
When I was the water deepest in the ocean.

What it feels like to be weak all the time?

I have been a weak child

A weak woman, a weak daughter

And a weak human being

Maybe I deserve to be as dark as the coal

As foggy as the morning fog

On a splendid summer, I deserve to sit still

Listen to what others have to say to me

Maybe I'm the clay molded into hundred different potteries

Maybe im the round the clock pointers

Returning to the same old dreaded place

Maybe I have forgotten how to be strong, free

For a bird who has been in prison

Wants to fly, but doesn't know how

Because it's a crime to be committed

Held by the rusty shackles of the self

I want to be applauded to be the one applauded for being strong

When the wide world shows me

How weak I am every time, everywhere I go.

I could have chosen to be white
But instead, I choose to be black
A color of shame
A color for the black sheep of the family
I could have chosen to be white
But I couldn't
Because I cant make peace in the world without any colors.

Spider Web

I have remained in a spider web
Sticking out my legs in a mess
I wondered whether I deserve it or not
To find out whether it is true or not

I laugh, I cry, I beg
Nothing happens
As the last flame of candle blows out
 I can smell the extinguished flame
In the roaring wind.

I keep quiet as I feel a slimy thing
Walking up my spine
I try to scream but I stop
I know it would harm me.

I couldn't cry, my hair spike up
In the darkness of the night
I can hear the howling of the wolves

I fear a break in the twig will break my silence.

I close my eyes, I shut out the voice
I feel the warm drops falling off my eyes.
I shiver with my jaws moving up and down
As I feel water underneath my bed.

Blessed

I'm so blessed to see the lime in the water float

As it removes all the negativity of the house

I'm so blessed to see the covers of the diary

Filled with funny numbers 77 44 11

I'm so blessed to see your arms

Inked in blue and green

With weird numbers 2450

All wiped off

I'm so blessed to see the nigella seeds

Spread out at each nook of the door

In our house

I feel so blessed to live with all the concerns of your wellbeing

That no words can describe

How the water in my eyes turn into an ocean?

I feel so blessed to live with an amazing soul

Like you

Who made me clenched my jaw

Made my headache worst with blessings.

I hear a drip, another drip, another drip

Till I run out of the room to the guest room

To see the plethora of colors becoming white in unison

The leaves falling down inside the verandah

The wind chimes dancing in joy

As the cool wind touches the face

I go outside with the drip, drip of water droplets

They touch the steel roof, the brick floors shamelessly

I rejoice in the moment with my hair dripping wet

My clothes hugging me tight

I close my eyes to feel the drip falling from above.

I love to see you play the flute

Whose melodious tune carried people to the shore

I love to see your huzz-buzz in your casual

When all of them seems to be a bit more extra

I love your smile, your presence, your laughter

I love walking down the street in some unknown corners of the city

With your hands on my hands

I feel all the amazing emotions of the world in one place

The walls around me crumble down

The cage around me is broken somehow

I love the me, when I was around you.

I love the me, when I remember all those memories with you.

Yesterday, I felt a cool breeze on my face
Toffees, toffees , toffees
Slapping on my head
I laugh and I try to look upwards
But my mouth is filled with chocolates
My hands are colored brown
I run away in fear
For I must have visited the Willy Wonka
Instead of the Drizzle-Dazzle.

Haiku 1

You have all you want
In the nature of cool breeze
Except peace

Haiku 2

Tiny drizzle on my head
All falling on my little eyes
Yet none touches the heart

Haiku 3

I never saw the snow
I never saw beyond my city
Yet I met with life.

Haiku 4

I love dates with friends
When we get-together at my place
I love them deseeded.

Tanka 1

The world turns dark within
Imaging laughter as my shroud
Losing the mask of grief
With no light and breathe within me
Joining the broken pieces of heart.

Poetry by Manmohan Sadana

Satnam

In the heart of New Alipore in Kolkata,
Lives a family of eleven, from Rawalpindi.
In their midst, a young boy, frail but handsome,
Afflicted with muscular dystrophy, is blessed.

Satnam a soul - pure is a beacon of divine light,
Whose body may disintegrate, but humour shines bright.

With each passing day, he faces his destiny,
But never-ever does his demeanour reflect his plight.

The family, a Persian tapestry woven with care,
Gathers around him, his inner pain to share.
Through trials and tribulations, they stand as one,
United by love, under the Kolkata sun.

His grandmother, weary from life's strife,
Finds solace in Satnam's resilient life.
Parents, uncle, aunts, and kin,
His laughter weaves them close within.

Bickering fades when his jokes arise,
Jealousies quelled by his twinkling eyes.
Siblings and cousins, once torn apart,
Find unity in his generous heart.

Through trials that seem too much to bear,
He teaches love beyond compare.
In his laughter, a bond is found,
In his spirit, love knows no bound.

So, in this home where love's the key,
A boy with humour sets hearts free.
Muscular dystrophy may claim his frame,
But his laughter leaves a lasting flame.

Satnam's laughter, a melody so mesmerizing,
Echoes through the rooms, a cure for the afflicted.
His wit and charm, a shield against despair,
Bring smiles to faces burdened with care.

In the courtyard, under the ancient banyan tree,
The family gathers, their spirits set free.
Satnam sits among them, his eyes all aglow,
As he spins tales of wonder, letting laughter flow.

With each joke and jest, he binds the family tight,
A beacon of hope in the darkest of night.
His laughter, a symphony of joy and delight,
Guides them through darkness, into the divine light.

Through his eyes, the cousins see the world anew,
Finding beauty in moments, both old and new.
Satnam's presence, a blessing so rare,

Fills the hearts of siblings with love beyond compare.

As the days turn into years, and time marches on,
Satnam's strength never falters, never gone.
Though his body may weaken, his spirit remains strong,
A testament to the power of laughter's song.

And so, in the heart of Kolkata, a family stands tall,
United by love, they'll never let fall.
For in Satnam's laughter, they find their way,
Together they will journey, come what may.

Poetry by
Kamalika Bhattacharya

Wish

Just a thought,

If I have a last minute to wish upon,

I would like to pray that,

when the next person calls you charming,

does in a way that encompasses all of you..

When they find you exquisite,

they mean your voice in the morning is as bright as a beam of sunlight,

and yet lit in the light of your eyes like twilight...

I hope when they admire you,

they see what you are passionate about,

hope they will find you adorable,

when you will sneeze and suddenly your nose will turn pink,

I hope they will find you cute,

even if you forget your keys everytime before you leave,

so you always say goodbye twice before you leave for work,

I hope they will like you the way you sleep,

the way you walk, the way you drink your coffee...

... Because next time nothing about you should remain disregarded..

And all this while I only tried to reach you with my words,

but it's not easy to love....

When I revisit my love notes for you

i see how gullible I am and scared of the fact

that you will fade away...

and again my soul will be empty.

I apologize for being so clingy...

but I will never regret loving you madly.

However, the door to my heart remains ajar,

And I can't deny of having

Endless fandom for you,

The simple reason of all of it is love…

No matter what...

Silent Storm

There is an overgrown tree near my place,

It stands as witness to my melancholy

Of moods, its huge size and open branches

often look at me as if they want to wrap me in its arms and tell,

so what things are not how you want them to be...

your heart is enticed by someones shadow who's not picture perfect either,

and yet you accept the love it brings...

We all learn to dance with devils,

Somewhere along the way to heaven....

You are not an fallen angel,

But yet everything about you feels flawless,

Your truth, your words, your being.

Even the parts you cast away...

Everytime my eyes became teary,

The universe knows something,

It knows i needed your light,

From sun to midnight...

And yet I remained hollow,
You never returned.

I don't mind kissing your insecurities...
The layers of love you offered never hurt,
because i learned to accept you in every way,
to look at you with love...
We fill our eyes with love to marvel at our beloved..
Like creepers trying to match their hands,
You are woven into each fiber
of my soul deep within..

Spot it!

You are the laughter that
echoes in the corridors of my heart,
In the silence of nights,
when I ride the chariots of yesterday,
I am crowded by your memories,
That distinct fragrance of yours.
My fingers still remember the   meadows of your face,
Those timeless curves of your lips,
And that tranquillity of
Your face...

Listen my love,
I want to remember you,
Long after the silverfish
would have eaten my youthfulness,
I want to recall your face,
the spark of your eyes,
the echoes of your voice calling out my name,
the crook of your arms,

the clasp of your hands on mine,
The arch of your dreams,
I barged into,
the butterflies of our first kiss,
The turbulence of my heart
When I surrendered

The light of that moment when we became US,
The wet pillowcases and my trembling lips Uttering your name,
The pain of the tattoo
inking our love,

A gaze of yours meeting mine,
Those silent pillow talks we shared,
Those lazy moments in each others arms,
Those bundle of love we know we have,
Those colours of sorrow we always hide,
That parting of hands when we said goodbye,
I want to remember you, A little longer than,
Your memory allows you to.
Just spot it and keep it safe.

Wordshore

I want to grew up as a kind hearted person, With sheer good intentions and no Expectations,

With less anxiety, and more divinity,

With less of blockage and more of forbearance.

With less disapproval and more solicitousness.

With less of hurt and more of gentleness.

With less of barbarousness and more of thoughtfulness.

With less selfishness and more graciousness. With less of harshness and more of tolerance, With less cruelty and affection.

With less of a disadvantage and more of benevolence.

With less meanness and more charity.

With less of obstruction and more of magnanimity.

 With less of hindrance and more of clemency.

With less hostility and more acceptance.

With less of indecency and more of beneficence.'

With less animosity and more tenderness.

With less of injury and more of succor.
With less pride and more amiability.
With less resentment and more assistance.
With less prejudice and more helpfulness.

With less of impasse and more of considerations.
With less of foulness and more of goodness.
With less of outrageousness and more of indulgence.
With less of coarseness and more of altruism.
With less of vileness and more of temperance.

With less of offense and more of endurance.
With less of greed and more of qualms.
With less of malice and more of regard.
With less of beastliness and more of compassion.

With less of covetousness and more of agreement.
With less of wickedness and more of responsiveness.
With less of pettiness and more of warmheartedness.
With less of unworthiness and more of affinity.

With less of apathy and more of generosity.
With less of detachment and more of bounty,
With less of listlessness and more of forgiveness.'
With less of disdain and more of humanity.
With undivided love and unparalleled feelings

Let's grow in eachother, for eachother.

Poetry by Aurobindo Ghosh

Nagoa Beach, Diu

I have loved the sand of many beaches like Dubai, Bali,

Baku, Sharjah and Abu Dhabi in the east, Amsterdam,

Venice, Kanes, niece and Montecarlo in the west.

All are extraordinarily beautiful but without much life.

In my India, Mumbai, Kolkata, Goa, Thiruvananthapuram,

Chennai, Kovalam, Rameshwaram, Puri, Digha, Chennai, Hazara, Daman, Somnath, Dwarka, Mundra and Nagoa.

They are not so extraordinary but full of welcome factor.

Recently, we both went to Nagoa in Diu in the west

Sheltered very near to the so called shiny sand of the sea.

Stretched over perhaps two kilometres in length in a curve.

It wanted to file nomination for both cleanliness and ease.

These beaches were there long before we evolved.

These sands were there glittering without foot smashes.

The water was cleaner not muddy and grey like now.

No boat and no pollution of petrol vehicles with noise.

In some hundreds and thousands of years passing by,

Men with power became the owners of natural entities.

They gained right to spoil the environment so crucial.

In the name of entertainment, sea was simply molested.

Adam said to Eve, "Darling, let us go to Garden of Eden,

To see the present status of the place of our expulsion".

When we were only two, the law and order was strict.

Code of conduct involving moral discipline were rigid.

"We were warned about Zero Tolerance", reminded Eve.

Adam said "Yes, we thought of God's big heartedness.

We had mistaken about our mutual behavioural trust.

Our faith on God's forgiveness was proved to be a myth.

No second chance was ever given to Adam and Eve.

They were expelled for a mistake committed unknowingly.

They were never given a chance to defend themselves.

There was no defence counsel system to protect them.

Adam remembered that he was alone in that garden.

God instructed "two" and commanded "one" to observe.

Firstly, create a beautiful atmosphere in the garden and

Secondly, plant a tree of forbidden fruits at the centre.

The command came far later when God created Eve.

Once Adam was asleep and God took a rib out of him.

From that rib, He made Eve to make Adam's companion.

When Adam awoke, he was delighted to find Eve standing.

He embraced Eve, kissed her forehead and started talking.

There was no time zone for them, only had Sun and Moon.

Full moon nights were special, they talked a little more.

They never ever forgot to obey the commandment of God.

"Never dare to think to pluck the fruit of the forbidden tree.

If you do so, instantaneously you both will be thrown out.

No second chance is available the in the Garden of Lords.

Never you will be allowed again to enter into this garden."

Who sent the serpent who induced Eve to convince Adam?

Why Adam was easily convinced that they would just taste?

Knowing well that the forbidden fruit was not to be tasted,

It was the command of God Himself, why it was broken?

The snake knew that the tree gives fruits of knowledge.

The snake also knew that ladies are always inquisitive.

That's why it chose to convince the lady than the man.

It was a sly move by an entity, also created by God.

It was obvious that once the lady becomes knowledgeable,

She will easily convince her partner to taste the fruit.

Till now, Adam was not Adam and Eve was not Eve.

They were only two different entities, created by God.

They both were ignorant about their being so important.

They never thought of the physical differences so vivid.

They both had no knowledge of anything, they were happy.

They hardly knew that source of unhappiness is knowledge.

The serpent did the trick of targeting the lady with a story.

"Do you know young lady that God Is jealous of you"?

It started with a questionable question to begin with.

"What do you want to say" Counter questioned the lady.

"Listen carefully. God does not want anybody like Him."

It said, "If you eat that fruit, you will be knowledgeable."

It also said, " ThenYou will be equally powerful like Him".

"God is afraid, You may dethrone Him from His seat."

She ultimately agreed to eat the fruit of knowledge once.

The serpent helped her to fetch the fruit from the tree.

She should not have forgotten the command of God.

She should have ignored the temptation to eat that fruit.

With the fruit in her hand, she was thinking about her man.

Should she eat first or would she ask her man to eat first.

The serpent knew well that, the man won't taste it first.

He will convince the lady, follow the command of God.

The serpent did not take any risk of spoiling its masterplan.

"Don't waste time lady, the fruit's power will not last long."

It cautioned, "If you don't eat now, you won't eat ever."

Hesitatingly, the girl tasted the forbidden fruit of knowledge.

She was delighted to have tons of knowledge eluded so far.

She ran to her man and gave her remaining part of he fruit.

She insisted him to taste the forbidden fruits of knowledge.

And he tasted to become the most knowledgeable person.

Both saw each other and found the difference to be hidden.

Suddenly God appeared, both ran behind the tree to hide.

God understood that His command was broken by both.

Instantaneously, He called the guard and gave His verdict.

"From this moment these two entities won't stay here ever.

From now on they will be known as knowledgeable mortals.

They will be loaded with Attributes, Intentions and Dreams.

They will now experience both happiness and sufferings."

They were out of the Garden of Eden, by the order of God.

A guard with sword of fire was assigned to protect the area.

No sooner they saw themselves, they covered their body.

For identification, named themselves as Adam and Eve.

They are knowledgeable now, they had many attributes.

Love, hate, anger, fear, nervousness, ego care, sympathy, jealousy, betrayal, boldness, leadership, dictatorship, sportsmanship, relationships, Friendship, craftsmanship.

Intense intentions added in the mind of Adam and Eve.

To satisfy themselves, they could now commit murder.

Other crimes, deceiving, alibi, protectionism, nationalism.

Now they will create their own language and religion.

Dreams came along with many attributes and intentions.

To be King or Queen, Dictator, Master, Ruler, Administrator.

Good dreams too were added like Writer, Warrior, Saviour.

It made collage of many Attributes, Intentions and Dreams.

Now they will be independent with fear of God or anybody.

They will have their own children, raise them as they wish.

May or may not see their grandchildren, they are mortals.

They have to go back leaving only their desired legacy.

Adam and Eve went out to find the "Garden of Eden."

They were expelled thousands of centuries ago by God.

Frantically they both searched everywhere on this earth.

But they could not find that beautiful garden, their home.

Instead they collided with heaps of garbage every where.

Oh My God!! Stinking dirt, "Houseful" Cinema hall and Jail.

Rush hour, Accidents, War zones, Volcano, Earthquakes.

Lightening, Tsunami, Forest fire, Floods, Weather change.

They found the children's children were weeping, unhappy.

Few flowers were blooming here and there as beauty spot.

Pollution of water and air were unbearable, made them cry.

The golden shiny beaches had become muddy and sticky.

Hatred all around in the name of Religion, Caste and Creed.

Gifted values of womanhood was crushed and humiliated.

Beautiful grasslands were converted into concrete jungles.

Oh dear dear!! Eve, why you listened to the serpent so evil!

Suddenly, they found a bunch of children laughing aloud.

Some were cleaning the field, some were planting plants.

Some were busy cleaning the nearby river so dear to them.

They were singing, "Let us create the "Garden of Eden."

They saw each other, they stopped and went near the field.

Adam and Eve heard the chorus, very clear and very sweet.

"We are the one, who care for this earth so lovingly made.

Together we will burry the misdeeds of the past so cruel."

One day they will surely bring back the "Garden of Eden".

Or the "Garden of Lords" or the "Garden of God" for sure.

Adam and Eve prayed , " O Lord, fulfil their dream please."

My wife woke me up, "Let us go to the beach for Sunrise.

About the Poets

Riddhima Sen

Riddhima Sen is currently studying comparative Literature at Jadavpur University. She is an author, artist and host.

Sabbani Laxminarayana

Sabbani Laxminarayana, a retired Junior Lecturer in English from Telangana, boasts an impressive literary career with 35 published books in Telugu ,spanning poetry, fiction, nonfiction, and prose. He writes in Telugu, Hindi and English. Some of his stories and poems have been translated into English and Hindi languages. Recognized for his academic and literary contributions, he has received awards such as the Best Teacher Award from the Government of Andhra Pradesh in 2013, P.S. Telugu University Award in 2018, and the "Nava Srujan Kala Praveen Award" Kanpur , U.P. in 2020. His patriotic contribution earned him the "Azadi ka Amrit Mahotsav" Desh Bhakti Geet State level Second Prize in 2022 for Telangana State. Acknowledged by the Telangana Book of Records with the "Best Writer Award" in 2023. He has authored 11 books and composed 6 songs on Telangana.He holds M.A. (English); M.A. (Hindi); M.Sc.(Psychology), M.A.(Astrology), M.Ed; and PGDTE qualifications. For inquiries, Sabbani Laxminarayana can be contacted via email at *In.sabbani@gmail.com* Or on his mobile +918985251271.

Rhodesia

Rhodesia is a multifaceted individual—a Filipina physician, past medical professor, past clinical and academic administrator, author, painter, and poet. At the remarkable age of nine, she was celebrated as the Philippines' Youngest Author for compiling an anthology of poems. While presently dedicated to being a loving mother of two, she continues to contribute to the well-being of others through teleconsultations, all the while reigniting her passion for the written word.

Revathi Raj Iyer

Ms. Revathi Raj Iyer is the author of: "Tales from Sri Lanka and India," "Syra's Secret—Diverse Short Stories from Siliguri, Singapore and beyond," and "My Friendship with Yoga." Her works of fiction has also been featured in the anthologies, 'Sweet Sixteen,' 'The Whispering Pages,' 'Dear Mom' - Volume3, 'Suenos-Chasing Dreams,' and 'Tales in the City' – Volume 1. Her stories, poems, book reviews and articles have been published in print and online media. Professionally qualified in Law and as Company/Chartered Secretary from India and New Zealand, Revathi is a content writer, editor, beta reader, panel book reviewer and yoga/fitness enthusiast. She enjoys writing short stories as she believes that fiction gives a chance to express and reimagine life. She lives in the vibrant city of Ahmedabad, India, with her husband, and continues to write enchanting stories. Readers may follow her page "Expression of Pearls" *https://www.facebook.com/chirminey/* or email her on *chirminey@gmail.com*

Sankalita Roy

Sankalita Roy is an author, an English Language Trainer and an animal welfare worker from Kolkata in India. She is on her mission to brainwash people with the beauty of life and sharing her thoughts as it is in an authentic way. Her debut book, Some Unbothered Truths has led her to win the award for the title 'Poet of the Year' and her anthology 'Kolkata Diaries' has led her to be the 'Best contributor' in the many volumed series. Her literary contribution has led her to be a part of several anthologies, blogs and magazines. Apart from this, her anthologies have been a part of the eminent book fairs around the world including Kolkata, Delhi, Frankfurt and Bologna in Italy. Please visit her at *www.sankalitaroy.com*.

Manmohan Sadana

Manmohan Sadana, a retired Joint Director General (Tourism) Government of India is an author, editor, actor and a mandolinist, whose novel – "Healing Strings" has won various awards which include the "Literary Titan Gold Award", "Golden Book Award", "Ukiyoto Emerging Author Award", "Certificate of Appreciation from Kerala Tourism Mart Society" and "Ukiyoto Book of the Decade Award". He has written many short stories which have been published in different anthologies and books. After superannuation from Government Service, he was a student of Persian for three years in St. Stephen's College, New Delhi and presently he is brushing his theatre skills as a student of renowned Director, Activist and Playwright, Mr. Arvind Gaur, in Triveni Kala Sangam, New Delhi.

Kamalika Bhattacharya

Kamalika Bhattacharya has authored poems, short stories, and editorials for a number of journals. Her work deftly combines passion, drama, and love. She has years of valuable professional experience and has worked for a variety of print and media companies. Her urge to travel motivates her to write down her thoughts and develop a range of storylines. She strives to communicate the gamut of emotions that exist in human life by providing the characters appropriate intonations.

Aurobindo Ghosh

Dr. Aurobindo Ghosh's remarkable journey spans academia, art, and literature. With a vast educational background in Statistics and Economics, he devoted 35 years to teaching and later became a principal in management institutions. Beyond academia, he emerged as a motivational speaker and personality development trainer, impacting thousands. At 65, he ventured into poetry and painting, expressing his artistic vision. Multilingual, his literary works range from poems to short stories in various languages. Despite being 75, his creativity thrives, evidenced by ongoing projects and academic contributions. Dr. Ghosh's life epitomizes continuous exploration and creation across diverse domains.

www.ingramcontent.com/pod-product-compliance
Lightning Source LLC
LaVergne TN
LVHW041541070526
838199LV00046B/1775